Even Though I Am Not There...

Sharing My Heart's Lessons
Vol 1

I Am Always Here

Tammy R. Wicks

Tidan Publishing LLC
P.O. Box 9482
Columbus, Georgia 31907
Tidanpublishingllc@gmail.com

Cover design and all illustration collaboration by Tidan Publishing LLC

Edited by Charles C. Killion

Scriptures marked as King James Version are taken from the King James Bible, public domain.

All Scripture quotations are taken from THE MESSAGE, copyright © 1993, 2002, 2018 by Eugene H. Peterson. Used by permission of NavPress, represented by Tyndale House Publishers. All rights reserved.

NEW INTERNATIONAL VERSION (NIV) THE HOLY BIBLE, NEW INTERNATIONAL VERSION® NIV®
Copyright © 1973, 1978, 1984 by International Bible Society®
Used by permission. All rights reserved worldwide.

Published 2020
Columbus, Georgia
Library of Congress Control Number (Pending)

Printed in the United States of America
Print ISBN 978-1-7353208-4-7 (Revised)
EPUB ISBN 978-1-7353208-3-0

TABLE OF CONTENTS

Even Though I Am Not There…I Am Always Here

DEDICATION

To God The Father, God The Son, and God the Holy Spirit.
It is in you that I live, I move and I have my very being
(Acts 17:28). Without you I am nothing, and because of you,
anything is possible! Thank you for your grace, your mercy,
for always forgiving me and cleaning up all my messes (over
and over again). Please continue to develop, correct and guide
me. I thank you for your ever-abiding love through your son
Jesus. May the inspiration you give me in words inspire lives
all around the world. Thank you Lord for ALL you have done
for me! Amen.

When I finally finished this book, it was 4:18 am one morning.
I thought it was ironic because one of my children's favorite
scriptures is Phil 4:19, "and my God shall supply all of my
needs according to His riches in glory in Christ Jesus. (NKJV)
A few days later, an old and dear friend offered to edit my first
book. Thank you Lord for supplying yet another need. Many
thanks to Chuck Killion and his family for availing your time,
talents and treasures to support me now, as you always have.

Last but not least, to my two precious & anointed gifts, Tiara
and Daniel. Tidan Publishing was inspired by, and named after
you both. It represents everything that you both possess,
tenacity, excellence, compassion, selflessness, love, kindness,
passion, wisdom, and it is infused with the Spirit of God. I
hope the many years of hearing me saying what I "was going"
to do, and then seeing the manifestation encourages you to
chase your dreams, no matter what anyone thinks. Trust God,
don't give up, always get back up, and keep pressing!
Look at God...I finally did it!!

Introduction

AND SO IT BEGINS ...

Being confident of this very thing, that He
who has begun a good work in you will
complete it until the day of Jesus Christ.
Philippians 1:6

And so it begins. This is my official writing, or should I say my published writing journey, Praise God!! I always knew this is where I would end up by the Grace of God! Now before you put the book down and say, "well that was a little arrogant," let me take a slight step back and share with you why I made that statement. Anyone who knows me, or has spent more than six months getting to know me can attest to my claim to one day write books...yes plural, books. I have also dreamed of being a greeting card creator, God has made that passion come true as well. God put some gifts in me a very long time ago; matter of fact, Jeremiah 1:5 says that before He formed me in my Mother's womb, He knew me!! How about that? He knew I would be talkative, a little quirky, laugh a lot, love Him immensely, love people...especially children...cry when I see other people cry, love to read, and love to eat.

He also knew that I would one day grow from a little child who wrote letters to my Mother about anything and everything...to a woman with a heart full of wonderful thoughts to share with the world through cards and books. I just took a long time to believe in myself, to shed the fears of what people would think about me, about my gift, about my thoughts, and just chose to trust and believe God. More importantly, I had to learn to not worry about pleasing people...it's not possible anyways as people change their minds too much! Keeping up with "the Joneses," why? Do we know what the Joneses did to get where they are, or do we know if the Smiths are suffering in silence and don't even have two nickels to rub together...you just can't please people! Gal 6:4 tells us to examine our own work...and it ends by saying not to compare ourselves with someone else. That simply is not your path. (more about that in Chapter 4). So when it is all said and done, I have shed this fear, I am carefully walking in my purpose and only worried about pleasing God!

So why write a book? It's simple, I had to follow my passions, and I had to be obedient and show God that the gifts He entrusted me with decades ago would be cherished and not wasted. I always end my blog entries with "....the world is waiting," I am taking my own advice and the wait is now over! The Bible says to leave a legacy for your children's children (Prov 13:22), my writings will be one of my legacies. Everything I write is God-inspired, God-infused, and it is my desire to write what inspires, heals, helps, motivates, encourages, strengthens,

3

and invokes the emotion of love. Oh, I also think that I am a part-time comedian, something else God put in me--just a quick disclaimer as you turn the pages.

When you think back to when you were a child, also if you now have children of your own, the "window of opportunity" for them to be a captive to their parents is about 17 or 18 years, anything else is a bonus from God. As a parent, I pray that my children will always seek my advice, enjoy my company, and appreciate my presence in their lives. As I am quickly on my way to having an empty nester (one on her way to college and one entering four quick years of high school), I can't help but think what we all say at some point, "where did the time go?". I feel like just yesterday I was waiting for my daughter to enter high school, and now I blink and she's now in college!! It's exciting, it's overwhelming, it's bittersweet, but overall these are proud moments that every parent thanks God for.

With all of that said, about a year ago, I started thinking about everything that I had not told my children, or maybe I spoke to them about it, but perhaps the "age appropriateness" of the conversation may have left some things unsaid. I thought about how I could capture all of those conversations in one place, but also how could I encourage other parents on this path as well.

Children become this "whole" adult person with ideas, thoughts, feelings, opinions, passions and dreams of their own. So while they are a captive audience, you only hope that you can broach the age appropriate subjects at the right time, in the right place, and that some of it sinks into their hearts. It does not quite unfold the way that we adults want or imagine, so if you are like me, you just hope and pray for another opportunity for the various critical chats.

Now I'm not a Child Counselor, nor are any of my degrees specializing in subjects specific to children or counseling. However, through all of my life's experiences, nothing has trained me more than my walk with God, a lot of prayers, and a lot of advice from wonderful friends and family members. Before I had children of my own, I had hundreds of first-hand experiences through the lives of others who entrusted me with their precious children. I grew to understand that everything doesn't work for every person, and with children, what worked yesterday on this child may not work today. I believe that God has given me a few things to share in this season. It is my prayer and my hope that instead of incomplete downloads, this book will become something very tangible to touch the hearts of my children, and to other children and adults who read my book. As adults, we will not always be around, but the God of our salvation will be. This book is a deliberate reminder that no matter what situation they face in life, God is always there.

Through this compilation of topics in the pages that follow, you will hear my fears, my joys, my challenges, some failures, and most importantly, my victories. By sharing my experiences, lessons, and my heart, I hope to touch and encourage others around the world.

Chapter 1

IT ALL STARTS AND ENDS WITH HOME

"Houses are created with gifted builders, tools, and precise plans. Homes are created with love, laughter, and, praying hands."
~Tammy Wicks

Over the years when I was growing up my dad was in the military so we traveled around often to different places. No matter how old we became, each and every time we heard the word "orders," we knew that meant it was time to move. It was difficult for us as children to hear this word because my siblings and I knew we would have to make new friends all over again, and we would be the new kid at school all over again, it was frustrating. We would say things like, "Move again, what?" and "Do we get a vote?" Even when my Dad received orders to Hawaii, we thought the separation from our friends was too great and couldn't get excited. This is where my dear Mama stepped in, she made everything an adventure, everything! She is what the young people these days call, "EXTRA." She took us to the library and we saw pictures of the new location or sometimes if my Daddy was fortunate enough to have literature from someone who was assigned to that location too (a "sponsor"), she would share that information with us. She made everything an adventure, and that made the moves more tolerable. I did not understand the importance of that creativity until I became a mother myself.

You see, back then there was no social media, no cell phones to call each other, every long distance phone call showed up on your parent's bill, so all you had was a letter. I was fortunate that some of my friends had a Mom who was also my Mom's friend, so I only had an occasional two or three minutes of catching up on the telephone, but not very often. So I began to write letters and send pictures to my friends. My Grandparents even indulged me and would purchase really pretty stationery for me, so I had to write them, too. My Grandparents were so sweet, my return letters from them often contained a little cash, the paper kind!! A couple of my siblings tried to cash in on that opportunity for the money (hee hee), mine was more about love, communication, and staying connected.

My letters became the topic of conversation, and apparently they were quite funny. I don't know if it was all the "big" words that I tried to use at my young age, mostly misspelled I am sure, but there was always a chuckle whenever they were discussed. My Daddy then purchased a pocket dictionary for me, it was ON then!! I'll come back to my "infamous" letters and dictionary later, but my point was communicating and writing were cultivated a very long time ago in me.

Some would say it was an environmental or situational atmosphere that created my love for writing. I will always believe it was God gently fertilizing and tilling my heart for the next phases in my life.

I also give my mother much credit for making every house we lived in a home. Yes, an H-O-M-E, there is a difference. Our home for us was comfortable, lived-in, fun, the hang-out where our closest friends were welcome, held the best of games when it was rainy outside, and where so many memories were created and cherished. Most of the time this was a modest home, but it had everything we needed and most of what we wanted. It was always full of laughter, discipline, understanding, and a lot of love. My mother and father had a way of focusing on each individual, at the appropriate time, and then treated us as a collective unit for other situations.

For instance, I used to collect rocks...all kinds of rocks...I don't know why, but I just did. My mother and father indulged with this Rock Collection until it came time to move. The military had weight restrictions based upon the size of your family and your rank. With that said, not only was I forced to pick out a few of my favorites, but the others would be thrown away, or so I thought. Well, to me, they were all my favorite rocks, it was difficult to choose, and it was always an emotional moment for me. So I picked a few out, my Daddy let me carry them in my backpack that we all had to travel, and I said goodbye to my precious collection. During this one particular move, I was unpacking my boxes at the new house and to my surprise, my parents had packed some of those rocks that I thought I said goodbye to...Reunion Time!!!! What was special to me looking back is that they saw the anguish in me trying to select a few and leave the others behind and decided to let me keep them anyway. They were important to me, so those silly rocks became important to them.

At some point, I grew out of my love for rocks, but I find myself looking at them as an adult from time to time...just being honest. What was my point? What I experienced is what I believe the role of a parent is. To know each of your children individually and collectively, to validate them, and to incorporate what is important to them along the way. Let me just add that the contents of my backpack were very eclectic. My siblings were concerned about snacks and their toys. I had books, journals, stationery, stuffed animals (aka my friends), and yes, a few of my rocks. It's a wonder how I managed to keep all of that stuff in there, but again, it was important to me, so it became important to them.

I believe that part of making your house a home is listening and connecting with all of the people in it, and even some of their things. I remember back in the 70's, visiting family members who had that special room that had plastic on the furniture. You all remember that room, right? For us it meant that you could not go in that room--and God help your soul if you were caught playing in that room. Now, plastic must have been the "thing" because a lot of people had it. I did not understand the concept. I agree, it kept things cleaner and dust-free perhaps, but for me what it really meant was sticky legs or crunchy legs--that's not fun! In the summer, if you had on a dress or shorts and were privileged enough to sit in that room, your legs would stick to the plastic. Likewise in the winter, if you had on a dress or pants, the plastic was colder and crunchier, therefore, winter brought about crunchy legs. I disliked both sensations, so I tried my best to avoid encounters with plastic covered furniture. Okay, I digress, let me bring it back. My point here is this, there were some rooms in homes I visited that were "off limits" when I was growing up. The boundaries had to do with the things in the room, not the people who visited it.

My parents never had that rule, and neither do I. I always felt that

there should be some boundaries, but I never wanted my children to

feel that I was unavailable.

I remember one time when I was speaking with a dear friend of

mine and we were talking about my daughter sleeping in my bed. I told

him, "she just won't stay in her own bed no matter what I do, she gets

up in the middle of the night and I wake up, and she's there." I

proceeded to tell him, "They say that it's not good for parents to let

their children sleep in their bed." He looked at me and said with

laughter, "who are they, who are these people?" He then proceeded to

tell me that I should do whatever made my children feel safe and

secure. There was so much freedom in that statement for me and I did

just that. Tiara left when she was ready, and Daniel....my dear GIANT

son Daniel, I had to kick him out with both feet!

All jokes aside, I believe what was shared with me, you have to

consider what makes your children feel safe and feel comfortable. My

parents allowed me to sleep with them when I had nightmares, or

whenever I made up nightmares just to sleep next to my Mama. When my Daddy was away on trips for the military, she would let me sleep with her. I was the baby, I thought it was my birthright, but that excuse wore thin after a while. I think my wild sleeping and kicking off the sheets occasionally, or so she said, also earned me a one-way ticket straight to my own bedroom! But for a while, they indulged me until I managed it on my own. At all costs, my parents made me feel safe, loved, and comforted at home.

Here is a precious letter that I found from my daughter that was written back in 2013, she was about 11 years old.

Tiara Wicks
8/12/13
1st Period

"What is your favorite room in your home and why"

"My favorite room in my house is the living room. I chose the living room as my favorite, because there were alot of good things and a lot of bad things that happened in that particular room. The living room is where we sit down, talk about our day, and watch tv together. I wish there were more hours in a day so I could say all the things I have to say. When my family sits down in the living room sometimes we laugh, we cry, and sometimes we've had a bad day so we don't say anything at all. My mom and my brother love me for me and that's all that matters to me the most. Sometimes after my brother goes to sleep. My mom and I have quality time together and talk about things that upset me or hurt my feelings that day. I love when I get to come home and be with my mom and my brother, because that is when I get to be myself and be loved for who I am. That's why the living room is my favorite room in my house.

I never saw this assignment when my daughter wrote it. I found it going through her old notebooks and cleaning out a room. My daughter is like me in so many ways and writing is one of her gifts and outlets. I was happy to read that she felt as if she could be herself at home. I was elated that she felt loved. I wish that there were not days that she felt "we said nothing," but who knows, that may have been by design, quiet is perfect sometimes. What was most important to me was that she felt validated and that she could share her feelings with me, that I was listening. This letter is a precious reminder to me of what is important to her even today, and she's 18! These critical points have not changed with either of my children. Thank God they still desire their undivided time with me. As a busy parent, this can be challenging. However, God gave me grace and continues to show me how to validate them both collectively, and individually without invalidating the other or comparing the two.

Today my daughter is fine just being in the same room with me, my son likes to wander off with the gaming system and disappear for hours. So we have "Family Staff Meetings," we pray together, we have Bible Study, Movie Night, just us three. Equally important is our one-on-one time, so if one had an event, I would try to do something special with the other. I always looked forward to the conversation from them when we all reunited. It was "game on" when explaining who had the best time--oh did they embellish, especially Daniel. All a part of rivalries I guess, I actually recall doing a little bit of that myself growing up. My Daddy was so set on not making one of us feel less than we each received presents on the other siblings' birthdays. Yes I said it, every birthday all four of us received gifts. Now our non-birthday gift may have been something smaller while the birthday boy or girl received something bigger, or multiple gifts, but we all received gifts.

My Daddy was not a very emotional person in my younger years, but he truly had his ways of making us feel special, loved and validated. When we got older, something changed in him and he would cry unashamedly at the drop of a hat. I guess when we became adults he finally felt it was okay to let his guard down from being the strong "super hero" father to being a normal human being. I feel privileged that today, at the ages of 14 and 18, my children will still come into the living room and say, "Can we watch this together?" or "Can I watch this show out here with you?" Of course I am happy to change the channel. After all, the older I get, I have less time for TV, and when it's on, it watches me more than I want. (Let's say that I sometimes blink very slowly--like 5 minutes at a time). It may even turn into them being in the Living Room, but their phones are very nearby, watching a video, liking a post, or answering a text. Nevertheless, I'm thankful for these times with my children in our Living Room. No matter how much clutter, no matter what towels sit on the couch that need folding, or even if you find some pillows out of place, it really doesn't matter. It is our Living Room, and that is where our hearts meet up!

What I gleaned from my parents was to make the most of everything that you have, wherever you have it, that is what makes a HOME. Protect your home, pray over your home, and pray over your family. These memories will last forever and the memories and ideologies of HOME will be personal, impressionable, and priceless for your children. I encourage you to make your home, your sacred place, your bubble, a playground, your precious corner of the world for you and your family.

Chapter 2

THERE BUT FOR THE GRACE OF GOD GOES ME

Each of you should use whatever gift you have received to serve others, as faithful stewards of God's grace in its various forms.
1 Peter 4:10

One of the things my mother used to always say when she walked by someone or drove by someone, or even if we were watching the news, "there but for the grace of God goes me." Or sometimes I would really get confused because she would change it up and say, "there but for the grace of God goes I." So as a child I would think, "uhmmm….why is she mixing up pronouns, and what does she mean by that anyways?" For as far back as my mind can take me I've never known her not to say this statement, she still says it today. Most often it was said in sadness, or sometimes in disbelief, but she always said it. I never asked Mama what it meant, I just started observing when she would say it and correlated it to the different times it was stated, and I began to understand the statement a little bit better. Then as I grew older, the statement became more alive to me. After joining the Air Force, I would hear her words play over in my head every time I saw a person in need.

I really began to talk with God, began to seek Him on a different level. The more I talked to Him, the more He taught me. I came to a point in my life when I went from having a surface relationship with God to an ankle-deep relationship with Him. What do I mean by surface? It's kind of like that neighbor you say you "know", maybe you know their last name, like "The Johnsons," and maybe you see their two children come and go, so you say, "Oh, those are my neighbors The Johnsons, they have two children." Then to take it a little further, you begin to see Mrs. Johnson and no Mr. Johnson, so you formulate in your mind, "Those are my neighbors, The Johnsons, I think she recently went through a divorce, it's just her and her two children." Then one day you see Mrs. Johnson at your children's school and you find out that Mrs. Johnson is married with no children, but she is raising her sister's two children for a year because her sister and brother-in-law are both military. One is on a deployment, while the other works night shift. So, they decided that it would be best for their children to live with their aunt, Mrs. Johnson. What is my point? Things aren't always as they seem and there is always a story behind the scenes. Everybody has a story and it is the fabric of who they are, or once were.

In the scenario above, one would not have known any of that background information about Mrs. Johnson. In order to really know someone, one must be willing to take the time to go deeper. So back to my point, as I began to really walk with God, I really understood and appreciated the grace of God in my life. In other words, I did not get what I truly deserved because of God's abundant grace, He's just that good meaning that I didn't get what I deserved, thank you Jesus! God's grace can be explained as God's unmerited favor--I did not earn it, God doesn't owe it to me, but He gave it to me anyways. This means when you really, really didn't work hard on that paper, but you still received a glowing score-this means when you were younger, and hung out with friends that your Mom and Dad told you not to hang out with; God was covering you with His grace.

Maybe those same friends were in a car accident, and instead of the car wrapping around the tree and killing me, I walked away from that accident, why? Nothing but the grace of God! We can all think of what <u>didn't</u> happen to us because of the grace of God! God's grace wakes me up in the morning, not an alarm clock. God's grace gives me breath in my body and enables me to walk, talk, and think, not because I deserve it, it's because it is His gracious plan for my life.

If you can tap into the grace of God, you will unlock the wisdom of your very being, and more importantly, of everyone around you. God will give you that grace because it is His desire for us to serve, and to give, and to bless others. He blesses us to be a blessing to others. God's grace has enabled me to sit and write this book, after years of starting and stopping, God has given me the grace and resources to finish what He put in me. In writing this book I am able to deposit into my children and those reading this book.

God bless you as you read the words from these pages and I pray that you will see the immense gift that is the GRACE of God. It is my goal to remind you of God's grace and have it become a genuine and consistent part of your prayers and thought life. Remember that we want the grace of God extended to us, therefore we must extend that same grace to others.

God's grace is awesome, incredible, unlimited, and immeasurable. When you understand that, then you will understand that without it you could be where others are. You could be the person sleeping under the bridge, in the line at the local shelter, riding the bus or walking because you don't have a car. My parents taught me that I am no better or worse than them, and we all need God's grace in our lives.

One split-second decision could alter someone's life forever. Maybe you got in the wrong car, went to the wrong house, or slept in the wrong bed that set off a chain of events that are now on your list of regrets. Maybe a bad relationship brought someone to their knees, maybe a friend betrayed you and now you distrust everyone and are labeled as a "difficult person" because you have no friends. I look back on all of these events and I say it was nothing but the grace of God that kept me.

Oftentimes we forget about God's grace as it is applied to others. My parents taught me to pray for someone rather than to judge them. Call it what you want, but it's a judgement. There but for the grace of God goes me, it could have been me. When you see a person looking unkept or a little tattered, instead of judging, just pray a simple prayer for them. They could be a victim of domestic violence, or have lost their job, or their home could have just caught on fire -- we just don't know. So rather than judge them, remember this one simple thing, "there but for the grace of God goes me". Say a prayer for them, offer help if The Holy Spirit leads you.

I've learned not to judge, and if I feel like I am slipping, I audibly apologize to God and move on to a different subject. We all have some "stuff" we are dealing with. I am confident that despite my wrong turns, God's Grace is my GPS, and He always forgives me and gets me back on track...RECALCULATING my route.

Choose to be compassionate, choose to be empathetic, choose not to judge, and instead exercise grace. Don't judge others unless you want that same standard applied to you. (Matt 7:1-3, KVJ)

I've learned that God didn't make "bad" people, but there are people who have made some "bad" decisions in life, pray for them because we have all been there. Someone else's bad choices may be more visible than yours, it doesn't make them any worse...pray for them. I've learned that when someone crosses your mind...pray for them, pick up the phone and call them. Don't hesitate because God could be using you to restore that person. You don't want to miss any of God's assignments, the rewards are so great!

Remember that everyone has the same opportunity as you to change. As I stated, we all have stuff, junk, baggage, whatever you want to call it, we all have it. When you understand that everyone has the ability to change, you are less likely to remind them of who they <u>used</u> to be, or what they <u>used</u> to do. Don't be one of those voices who want to play the video of someone else's past.

This is the same for an adult as it is for a child. Let's say an adult made some bad choices, maybe the choices landed them in a very bad place in life. What if that same person works really hard, struggles, fights to position themselves in a better place only to have "voices" remind them of what they did, who they did it with, and how bad off they were? Who wants to hear those voices? No one!

Not only do they NOT want to hear those voices, they don't deserve to hear those voices. If God forgives and does not hold it against us, why do we hold things against others?

I'll end this chapter with this--everybody has a story, and it is the fabric of who they are, or once were. Exercise grace, just as God does daily with each one of us.

Chapter 3

SUPERNATURAL "OPEN" HEART SURGERY

Keep thy heart with all diligence; for out of it
are the issues of life. Proverbs 4:23

When God created us, so many intricate processes were considered. When I read about different components of our body and how things work on a granular level, it makes me not only thankful, but in complete awe of the magnificence that IS GOD Himself!!

Right in the center of our body is a precious, complex, integral muscle that is known as THE HEART! This incredible organ was created with four chambers and beats around 100,000 times a day. After researching further, I came across an article in The National Geographic that says the heart has the capacity to pump FRESH blood, oxygen and nutrients, while CLEARING AWAY, harmful waste matter. That is a lot of responsibility for one organ!

When I look at this in a metaphorical way, it's almost like God was trying to tell us that there would be things, situations, or people, that would be hurtful or harmful to us. In the same way our body involuntarily clears harmful waste matter, I recognized that I had, and periodically have some things in my life that need to be "cleared away" so it does no harm to me. He knew what I needed, and He made provision for us in advance. The Bible says that "out of heart flows issues of life" (Proverbs 4:23), so we are to guard it.

Luke 6:24 also says "...for it is out of the abundance of the heart that the mouth speaks." I have learned from a spiritual perspective, when your heart is clear, that is what will flow out of your mouth--clarity, joy, peace, freedom. Contrarily, when your heart is hardened, sick, angry or evil, that is also what will flow from you.

So I thought to myself...what have you allowed to enter into your life and into your heart that needs to be cleared away? What is flowing from your mouth? Words of life, words of encouragement, words of optimism, words of love? Or are they words of doubt, negativity, pessimism or fear? I had to flush some things away. I found myself saying, "I shouldn't have said that?" or "why did I say that?", or this is the one that I've wrestled with all of my life, "that didn't exactly come out right."

Just like when the arteries of a heart are clogged, medical intervention is required, I had to ask God to perform spiritual heart surgery on me. You see, my heart had some scars. It may have been a failed relationship, hurt feelings here or there, throw in some disappointments or betrayals, and this was a recipe for a nice hardened heart. You don't recognize it because it can happen over time, and before you know it, callousness sets in due to the scars and no one can enter in, not even God. This is a dangerous place to be in. Fortunately, my scars were not too hard for God, and He kept performing surgery. As one scar healed, He dealt with another, then another, and then another until I started to see what was happening in the Spirit realm. I am still healing, but I am diligently and deliberately persistent about my healing. It was baby steps at first, can I trust again, can I love again, am I offering my very best, or am I being cautious with walls up. The answer was, and still is, *"God please don't allow my heart to be hardened towards the things of God and towards people or situations, work on my heart."* I had to really stop and take inventory of what my heart was holding, and moreover, who was holding my heart. The word heart, or derivative of the word heart is mentioned approximately 300 times in The Holy Bible. What does that mean? God is absolutely concerned about the condition of our hearts. I've learned to practice what I want to produce in my life, and that is a clean and open heart. This is not always easy, but when it is done with the love of God, it becomes a part of your life.

Have the offenses or occasional offenses stopped, of course not, we are human and things happen. However, what God's grace has changed in me is that I don't allow people to enter my heart so deeply that the wound will take forever to heal. Those that enter in are tried by The Spirit of God, and I can trust them with my heart. Those that are in striking distance may land a blow, but it doesn't wipe me out any longer, the hurt doesn't linger, and it definitely does not create a scar that can later multiply and form a hardened heart, only greater grace and peace from God.

When people think of our hearts, we think of love, being in love, we think of trust, intimacy, a very closely held space that is the center of our being. Yet, it's not always treated with that importance. Hearts are also where we keep things, our secrets, our emotions, our dreams, our fears, it's ironic that the heart has "chambers", because it's where we securely store things. A judge's office is called a chamber, and yet, this is also where we tend to judge others, in this same precious heart. Such a complex and important organ, but do we place that priority on our heart?

My advice is to guard your heart, that's what God's Word tells us to do. Not everyone or everything is valuable enough to take up space in your precious heart. Sometimes people or situations will "break" your heart; don't be afraid to walk in wholeness and freedom. When your heart is broken, pray, seek wisdom and counsel that will help your path of emotional healing. Diligently seek to handle the hurt quickly, don't let it fester or harden, it will change who you are without you realizing it.

Meditate on what's in your heart, purge those things that are not good, and embrace and enhance those things that are positive, peaceful, loving, and that bring you joy. Lastly, let the love of God flow through you because your life is depending on it, so treat it with that priority and incredible importance.

Chapter 4

THAT'S NOT MY PATH

For I know the plans that I have for you, plans
of good and not evil, plans to prosper you and
give you an expected end. Jeremiah 29:11

Back in November of 2016, I had an entire book drafted titled "That's NOT My Path." I had named chapters and just knew that would be my first book. Well, things just happen sometimes and then I knew it was not supposed to be my first book. I may dust it off one day, but for now, I would just like to share my heart on this one particular topic. Have you ever found yourself saying, "I wish I could do that," or "I would love to be a this or a that?" More specifically have you found yourself wanting to do this or that because it's really what YOU want to do? Moreover, is the desire rooted in a place where you want to do it because someone else did it or is doing it? Are you doing it because you believe it is your gifts, your calling, your purpose, for the money? Why do you want what you want? I am not taking a stance here saying not to do something that someone else is doing. My goodness, I am writing a book, we know that millions of authors exist, right? What I want to convey is that YOU have to be confident in WHY you are doing what you are doing.

You should consider having a mission statement for your life. Without one, you will find yourself being indecisive, frustrated, and feeling some sense of inadequacy and insecurity all because you are not sure what you are sure of what you should be doing. I have been writing books for years, ask any of my friends who have known me for longer than 15 years, they will tell you my heart's desire is to be an author. I have prophecies that were spoken over me, the oldest one going back to 1992. So one may ask, what in the world have you been doing? My response is very simple, I was working on me. I was going through some processes. I was in training. It was not time.

All of those things are true, and at some points in my life, one may have been truer than others. Most of all, I had to figure me out and how to get to the place where I could operate in the gifts God has given me. I had to figure out why I was here, I mean fully figure it out. When I did, the fear left, the insecurity left, and I have squared my shoulders, planted my feet, gathered all my journals and said, "I'm ready now God, let's go!"

Because of that declaration, my prayers are in alignment with my purpose, my heart is fixed on manifestation and multiplication, I have spoken things out of my mouth that others are holding me accountable for, instead of keeping things to myself. It was a process, and it was not easy, but it is so worth it and I am ready to take on what

God promised me I would accomplish in this world, for His glory.

So I need you to ask yourself an audible question, "What are

you here for?" This is not a one time ask, I encourage you to ask it

often and audibly of yourself, and of God. There is a divine purpose in

you, what is that? Discover that, and you will innately understand and

begin innately understand and begin to connect the dots of the path

that God has mapped out for you. In life it's very easy to get deterred

or off your track. It's very logical to think "if I follow the

same or similar path that he/she did, I could end up having that

same life." That is just not so. Let me add a little clarity, I am

not speaking of a mentor/mentee type relationship here. Mentors

are powerful and necessary forces in our lives and the right mentor

can be a "midwife" in your path and push you into your destiny. My

recommendation is for you to find a few of them to provide counsel

in different areas of your lives. I am specifically referring to the

thought of emulating someone with an expectation of the obtaining the

same results. The same thing may not work for you because like a

great recipe, one may add an extra pinch of this, or may cook something in a different pan, it won't be identical every time. Likewise, you were given a path, a destiny, a plan for your life; before the foundation of the earth was created, God knew you! (Jer 1:5 and Jer 29:11). Isn't that AWESOME!! Why not try those shoes on for size? I assure you they will be a perfect fit for YOU!

You see it's not extremely awkward for a person to see something someone has or something someone is doing and say, "I would like to do that." I have done it myself, "Wow, I would love to write a book and have it featured on Oprah's Book Club," or "Wow, I would love to move people's spirit with the words I place on the pages of my books the way that Bishop T.D. Jakes does." I have not said I want to be like this person or that person and be on Oprah's Book Club, I want that for myself. It's on my Vision Board; I am praying am praying about it and if God chooses it for my life, it will come to manifestation. God has given this person or that person a special anointing. I can't try to walk in that person's anointing, I have my own to walk in, their path is not mine. You can end up at a similar place, but you have to walk through your own steps and your own process.

Let's talk about the process for a minute...my process may
not be your process. Why? We are different people with different
circumstances, with different resources, with different lives. I may have
made 35 stops over 12 years to write one book. You may have had
a wonderful dream, great inspiration, and published your book after
30 diligent days! Life works just like that. Why? We all have our own
process, our own decisions, our own circumstances, our OWN
PATHS! This is what makes us awesome as individuals.

When we put those differences together, we are able
to produce creative, incredible synergy that makes this world go
around. You cannot be envious of those who are more diligent than
you; however, you can use their success to motivate and elevate your
thinking about what is possible. Remember, they are walking in a
different anointing than you are because God gave us all some different
stuff! You don't need my stuff...God gave you your own stuff!! Your
gift can be similar to someone else's gift, but God put that special spin
on yours that makes you stand out in a different way. Don't try to do it
like him or her because you will miss out on your special spin!
I love reading autobiographies about people, partly because I am very

curious, (call it nosy, but it's my book, so I will say I am "curious"). The most exciting parts of any autobiographies are the comeback and success stories. There are always more happy endings than sad endings. There are common threads that bind them are, they are in every story, just look for yourself. You will find some heartache, failures, and disappointments, but you will also find tenacity, focus, discipline, vision, endurance, and last but not least, you will find that after a failure or when they fell short, they paused. They took an inventory, squared their shoulders, changed some things or people around, and they took off on their path once again.

For me, I have stepped away, put this book down, picked it back up, started three more books while completing this one, all to return to this as God gave me inspiration. I encourage you to keep God in the equation through prayer. He will center you, inspire you, encourage you, and download an entire book concept to you in 15 minutes. Ask me how I know! My heart's desire is for everyone to seek and find their OWN path, it's paved with specific instructions and situations just for YOU. Great joy, peace, and fulfillment comes when we follow the path created for you. Go...the world is waiting!

That's Not My Path

Chapter 5

EVERYONE DOES NOT WANT TO SEE YOU WIN

Bless your enemies; no cursing under your breath. Laugh with your happy friends when they're happy; share tears when they're down. Get along with each other; don't be stuck up. Make friends with nobodies; don't be the great somebody. Romans 12 :14-16

Life is full of harsh realities, and this is one of the hardest chapters of this book, but it must be said. Everyone does not want to see you win...let that sink in, because it's true. I believe the younger generations call it being a "hater", also known as a naysayer, being jealous, having a jealous spirit..oh yes, it is truly a spirit. Call it what you want, but the underlying behavior that exists is that there are people who don't want to see you win...PERIOD.

Some of this is learned, but more often than not I have found that competitive atmospheres and bitter spirits can manifest into the hater mindset. This mindset can be hurtful, divisive, destructive, contagious, and sometimes it is downright ridiculous, but it exists. I will even go so far to say this, are you ready?

DO NOT think that haters are restricted to people "outside" of your family...this spirit of hating knows NO BOUNDARIES, HAS NO LIMITS, and HAS NO RESPECT !!!

Now before I go any further, let me define my definition of a HATER. Someone who has a "hater" spirit is not necessarily someone who is jealous of you. They don't want to be you; they don't even want exactly what you have. My definition of hater is very simple, **THEY**

JUST DON'T WANT TO SEE YOU WIN...on any level. They cannot celebrate you, they cannot congratulate you, it may even disturb them to see others congratulate you. They are often attention seekers who cannot sit by and allow someone else to have more attention or mention than them. Haters are sometimes hard to spot, but trust me, they are there--that spirit is there. Haters come in different forms:

Obvious Haters - They can't and won't celebrate you, as a matter of fact, they are not capable of celebrating anyone but themselves.

Undercover Haters - They smile in your face and congratulate you, but they really don't believe in you. This type of hater may surprise you and I believe they can be close to you. This type of hater can be a friend in your social circle, a family member, or they may even be a co-worker, but they don't believe in you, nor can they celebrate you unconditionally. Any celebration is a fabricated surface celebration, but if you could look inside their heart, they are in private protest of your achievements.

Part-time Haters - They can celebrate you when things are going well for them, but if your happy moment even appears to be a bit happier than theirs, there is a problem. Their celebration is situational.

The Just Because Haters - This type of hater has no reason at all to not want you to win, they just don't want you to. They may not even be close to you, they may not understand why you do what you do and the sacrifices it took to get there. Matter of fact, they probably don't even care; they are just there to "nay-say" just because.

The One Up Hater - This type of hater is so incredibly obvious because no matter what someone else does, they have done it bigger and better. If you climbed a mountain, the mountain they climbed was much bigger. If you took a cruise, their cruise was longer and on a bigger boat. If you both were at the same concert, they had VIP tickets, backstage passes and they went to the afterparty. The reality is, they've never climbed a mountain, they've never sailed on a cruise ship, and they never went to the concert. In an effort to be bigger and better, the stories become grander, and all credibility is lost...all for what? To be the best at any cost, even if it means making things up.

What I find interesting about the hater behavior is also where compassion kicks in, and the Grace of God takes over. I am reminded that I may have been in one of those categories at some point in my past, so I should extend compassion and grace when I run into the haters today. What my adult self now knows is what my younger self did not understand. I have always taken it personal, however these behaviors have nothing, and I mean nothing to do with you or what you are doing. You are operating in the Grace and Favor of God; you can't apologize for those blessings. If they are mad with you, allow them to take that up with God. Their issues are really not your issues, so don't take their issues on, just pray for them.

Some people are fundamentally wrong in their righteousness, but they can't see or think clearly, so their reality is a little skewed. Just remember, you cannot change anyone else's behavior, you can only adjust how you react to them, and of course pray for them. What I've discovered is that the behavior normally has something to do with a missing piece within them. Maybe it's an insecurity or challenge that they are dealing with and they see you seemingly succeeding in the very thing they struggle with. Maybe they want to climb that mountain, maybe they want to go on a cruise and never have, maybe just maybe they saw the concert on TV and want others to believe that they were backstage with your favorite performer. God only knows why, but your mandate from God is to pray for them, don't just pray for those that love and support you. We are reminded to pray for our enemies always. (Luke 6:28) Pray for their hearts so that God can perform Supernatural Open Heart Surgery on them, pray for their brokenness to heal, and pray for their emptiness to be filled with the love of God.

When God is the compass guiding your heart, you have the capacity to love others as He loves you. At this beautiful juncture, there is no room to be the giver of "hateration". If you are the recipient of "hateration", you are so full of joy, love, and the peace of God, you don't stay in a place of concern long...instead you pray.

The takeaway here is, in life everyone is not going to like you, and everyone is not going to celebrate you, and that is completely O.K., it really is! Seek after God's validation and endorsement, that is the real gold standard! Over the years, God has surrounded me with such an amazing group of family and friends who celebrate me, love me, support me, lovingly correct me, ground me, protect me, and I feel safe with them. I am truly so blessed and so very grateful for them.

I close this chapter with this, remember to thank God for the Favor in your life, humbly walk before others, and pray for those around you..everyone! Keep and strengthen your firm foundation in Jesus, He will make it easier to navigate through your seasons of rough terrain, and in everything, remember to not allow anyone to steal your joy, for it is your strength! (Nehemiah 8:10)

Chapter 6

EPIC FAILS

Before his downfall a man's heart is proud, but humility comes before honor. Proverbs 18:12

Epic fails. Please note that I didn't make a grammatical error here, I purposely put an "s" on the end of the word "fail" because there will be many in our lifetime. As an adult, my children were integral in teaching me humility, why? They would boldly point out my mistakes, misspelled words, or how many times I did not not fully come to a stop at a stop sign. I look back on so many moments that leave me saying, "that didn't go so well", or "perhaps this wasn't the best time to have that conversation." I have spent many nights crying, venting to a close friend or family member, and praying about how to handle a particular situation. No one sets out to fail at anything, it is not our intention, but it does happen because we are human. The only one that never fails is God, and that is what has kept me through the good and the bad decisions, my ability to forgive myself for my missteps, especially in parenting.

Most of the time I find myself trying to practice prevention with my children, only ending up having to pursue prayer and protection because sometimes they want to go it alone and explore a different option than what I advised. My children are and have always been obedient, but that does not mean they did everything I asked of them to the letter. I didn't do it with my parents, and I would venture to say without statistical data, no child does EVERYTHING they are told. My goal was for my children to do the right thing even when no one was looking, especially me. I learned a long time ago that telling my children "no" or "because I said so" was not enough, it only frustrated them. So I decided years ago that when it was applicable, I would always try to sit them down and make that "no" into a teaching moment instead of something where they walked away frustrated or upset because they were just told "no." Likewise, when I botched something, I had that same sit down with them, sometimes embarrassed, and made the moment into a teaching one. I had to let them see that their mom was flawed, I had to let them see that their mom makes mistakes. Most importantly I had to let them see how their mom navigated through those mistakes.

For example, one time when I went to a big department store, I won't name names here, that would just be petty, but back to the story, I had purchased several items of clothing for my children. Tiara and Daniel were both in elementary school, but they were definitely old enough to understand the happenings around them. On this particular visit to said unnamed store, I visited with the specific intent of returning some children's clothes that did not fit. I didn't realize that when those items later went on sale, the max I would receive for those items would be the sale price. To this day I do not like to return items to the store. When the lady explained this to me, I was friendly, but I definitely asked to speak to her supervisor, and then the Store Manager. I didn't even want the money back, a store credit would have sufficed, however, I felt very cheated in the situation. I may have paid $19.99 for the blue jeans and they wanted to issue me a credit of $6.99, I was not having it. Well, one of the members up the chain was not very nice, matter of fact, they were a bit condescending and it got way under my skin. He quoted some ridiculous rule, I brought them back outside of a window, on and on and on.

As I grew more and more annoyed, I said a few choice words that embarrassed my son. They were not curse words, but I was speaking with a voice a lot more elevated than Daniel liked. The team member was not budging and I refused to leave them with my "new tag still on them" merchandise without a satisfactory credit. Daniel sat patiently in a chair while I went to my different iterations of annoyance because in my mind I wanted my full credit they just were not willing to give it to me. So I think I ended the conversation with, "before I let you give me the seven-dollar credit for what I paid full price for, I'll take it to Goodwill", and that's exactly what I did.

Now, I would rather have donated those new items than receive the credit, but looking back it really was so silly. I just wanted to be right, I let my pride get the best of me, and most importantly, I displayed it all in front of my precious son. I wanted things to go my way that day and it did not happen. The issue was so insignificant and it wasn't my best self, matter of fact, I was just wrong in all of my righteousness! I was so caught up in being right that I thought my son was looking at his hand-held video game, however, he was not. He was watching every second of my movement and Lord only knew what he was thinking or saying to himself. I know that he was not proud, but he just looked at me and we left the store. No discussion about the matter, nothing, we just left. Actually, to make matters worse, I boycotted the store for a whole year until I really needed something they placed on sale.

On that return trip as we pulled up to the store and parked, we got out, and began to walk towards the store, thinking about the delicious popcorn and another treat that we were going to purchase. Before we could get to the entrance, my son looked at me and said, "Mommy please don't go in here and show out like you did last time." What?! Did he remember that?! Daniel was probably five or six, but a year later he remembered exactly what happened. Mind blown -- EPIC FAIL!

So when we got into the store, I had a little chat with him that started with, "Son, I am so sorry that I gave you that type of memory. That was not a good look, that was not one of Mommy's proudest moments." After that incident, instead of allowing things to linger, I always turned them into teaching moments. I witnessed my son unnecessarily hold onto a memory that wasn't very nice for a year. As we speak, if we are somewhere and anyone is rude about anything, Daniel will tap me or tug on my shirt and say things like, "Mommy let's just go", or "Mommy, please don't say anything to them." He is a Godsend! Tiara is no drama at all, N-O-N-E! I had to ask God, where did these two children come from, and they are mine, like, are you sure?!!! Needless to say, over the years, they have taught me just as much as I have taught them.

There are so many additional examples that I can provide, but the point that I want to convey here is that it's harmful to allow a bad memory to take root, fester and grow. As parents, please don't do what I did and allow your failures, big or small, to create bad memories, flip them and make them a teaching moment. All that it requires is truth, humility, and your willingness to have a great conversation. My children walk a little more quietly and calmly than I do throughout the world.

They get excited or passionate about something, but the loudest thing that they both have is their laughter, and I absolutely love that about them. I am certain that God sent them to balance me. Yes they have their moments, but they have made me adapt and adjust; but I also have also taught them to live life to the fullest...to be silly, to have fun. I have truly learned that anger is an emotion. It's an emotion that God gave us, even the Scriptures say to be angry, but to sin not (Eph 4:26).

Over the years, I have identified my triggers and if you know them, the devil knows them and will stand by flipping that switch on and off occasionally. What we have to do is pray through those tough moments where we have to make a decision to blow up on someone, or to slow up! I do this by reminding myself what it is to operate in the Fruit of The Spirit (Gal 5:22-23). These characteristics guide me and bring me back to a sweet, centered place. When I am operating in love, joy, patience, kindness, peace, goodness, faithfulness, gentleness, and self-control, this will help to minimize my failures and increase my successes.

As we speak, my children will come to me with what they believe are challenges or pending failures, I believe that it's by God's Grace they are able to do that, and because of my ability to say, "I'm sorry," "I was wrong," "That was a bad decision on my part." This allows them to be human, fallible, and negates all attempts of anyone to isolate them due to any type of failure. This way, failures are viewed less monumental, and more manageable.

I leave you with this, failures are a part of life, we will all have them in every area, we learn, we grow, and we pray that we make better decisions in our futures. No regrets…just lessons. With children we have no handbook or manual other than the Word of God. There are hidden treasures we tap into when we pray and ask God for

His wisdom concerning our children. One of the nuggets God has given me is to make a practice of listening to my children's hearts, instead of only listening to what is coming out of their mouth. This will lay the foundation for a unique and wonderful relationship consisting of honest, humble, trusting, and healthy conversations.

Chapter 7

THE POWER OF WORDS

Death and life are in the power of the tongue and they that love it shall eat that fruit the fruit thereof. Proverbs 18:21

The Power Of Words

Over the years I have heard so many people say "words are so powerful." As I grew older, I began to understand how incredibly right that statement was…and still is today. Very simply put, we are what we say we are. We have what we say we have. We can do what we say we can do. It all comes back to, and starts with, the words that you release. Words speak destiny, they speak life, they can create your wildest dreams, and they can tear one down...all because of words. Knowing the gravity and weight that words hold, we have to hold our tongue more accountable.

The Bible is loaded, I mean packed. with advice about our words and our tongue. If our words were not that powerful, I just don't believe that it would have been referenced so many times in the scriptures. Even the Bible says that we overcome the enemy by the blood of the Lamb, that's Jesus, and the WORDS of our testimony. (Rev 12:11) Our words have power, they mean something, let's activate some things in our life with our words!

I challenge you to think about what "right" words can do in our own lives, but especially in the lives of others. If we can just lay hold of this one powerful principle, we can build so much by just being accountable to our words. As you may have gleaned by now, when I was young I loved to read and write. My mother used to take us to the library, and I was appreciative, but you had to return those books. So I often would find myself negotiating with my parents to purchase something from the Scholastic leaflet that our teachers used to pass out. Some of you will know exactly what I'm talking about right? I would even save my own money just to buy these books. I went from that to my Daddy purchasing these read-along books, they would have a cassette tape and when it was time to turn the page, there would be a loud "beep". I would listen to them over and over again, reading along, but there was something about hearing the words that brought the story more to life!

Then one day, my Daddy came home with a small pocket dictionary. It was white with a plastic cover, and the words were really, really small, but that didn't matter to me. He challenged me this: for every word that I learned, the spelling and the definition of the word, he would pay me a dime. I tried to earn as many dimes as possible. Even when it was "test time" and I collected my change, if I didn't quite get one right, I didn't quit. I made sure that I reviewed those particular words again first, and cashed in on those the next time! My Dad is in Heaven now, passed away in 2015. However, I pray that he is smiling down on me knowing that God used him to plant and cultivate what was deep within me by purchasing that dictionary and motivating me to expand my vocabulary. He too knew how powerful words were, and still are.

Back to accountability, when I say we have to be accountable for our words, I really mean we have to be prepared to accept the world we create with our words. If you call your child "bad" all of the time, and then you receive calls at work from your child's school because he is misbehaving, remember what you called them. If you say to your child, "I don't think you are good enough to do that," then they won't be.

As an example, my son Daniel has always been very petite for his age. He was normally the smallest child in the class, and he normally was greeted by all of his teachers with a sweet smile telling him how adorable, cute, and little he was for his age. Because Daniel was so small, I began to call him my "GIANT son." I would say things like, "Wow I think you have grown an inch this week," or "come here my GIANT son." I spent extra time telling him how he was just as good as those taller than him; and even more so, I would share the Bible Story of David and Goliath. Well, perhaps I did this a little too much. At one point, Daniel got his "sea legs" and was feeling himself a bit. Allow me to sidestep a moment for a quick story about my GIANT son.

There was a young man that liked to pick on Daniel...he may have been in the 2nd or 3rd Grade when this encounter happened. I don't recall how many times that Daniel came home and spoke to me about it, but it was at least two. On our third discussion, I stated the same thing, "Please speak to the teacher about it," but this time, I added that I would be contacting the teacher as well if it continued. You see, there was no physical contact, but there were "words" that he kept launching at Daniel daily, all centered around him being so small and short, things of that nature. I used to teach my children what I was always taught, "sticks and stones will break your bones, but words will never hurt you." Well, that all changed quickly!! Words absolutely do hurt, they can break your heart and impact your self-esteem.

Back to my story, that next day when I picked Daniel up from the After School Program, he had a different pep in his step. As always, I asked him how his day was, and we went through every high and low, to include what he ate for lunch. When we arrived home, I began to make dinner when Daniel entered the kitchen. He said, "Oh yeah Mama, the teacher may be contacting you about something." So I wanted to know what the teacher "may be contacting me about," what did he conveniently forget to tell me? He explained that the same kid who had been bothering him threw a basketball straight in his face! I screamed, WHAT!!!!!???? Mama Bear came out in .02 seconds. "Daniel, what happened, what did you do, are you okay?!!!" Daniel calmly said, "Oh no Mama, don't worry about it, everything is fine." I am looking at him and he calmly explained, "You see I called my Dad yesterday and he told me if that kid put his hand on me, to ball my fist up really tight and punch him right in the middle of his face, so that is what I did after he threw the basketball at me." So I was frozen, but quiet. I was hesitant because I just knew I was headed for a parent-teacher conference the next morning. I said, "Son, what happened next?" He said, "Oh nothing, he just got up and walked away...limping!" As he told the story, he demonstrated how the other kid was dragging his leg.

Full transparency...I laughed really hysterically! Partly because of the portrayal by Daniel, then partly because he had stood up for himself. He never told me the young man's name and I never asked. I just waited for the call from the Principal but it never came. Deep down I believe that God was looking out for my GIANT son and spared him the discipline that time around. We of course had a conversation about not being a bully, but most importantly, not being a victim. Because the words escalated to a physical level, I definitely did not punish him, but that incident shifted my thinking on words to a new level. That GIANT that I had spoken over my son since he was young had manifested in his heart and his spirit, and he landed a pretty good punch. While that was not the desired outcome, hurting another child, I think you receive the point. Call your children what you want to see manifest in their lives.

People can be cruel and mean-spirited with their words, but I choose to believe that most people truly just don't understand the POWER of their words. If we truly believed the words we spoke had power, we would be more accountable to our own tongues.

I challenge you to reflect on your own choice of words and affirm yourself, start with Y-O-U.

This is a great way to condition your tongue when you are speaking to others, especially your children. Make a deliberate choice to hold your tongue accountable! It's a rewarding and liberating feeling to speak life, to speak destiny, to speak greatness, to speak success, to speak healing, to speak comfort, to speak victory! Throughout this book I have referenced several scriptures that have helped me grow and understand more fully the power we possess with our words, and the importance of holding our tongues accountable.

There is a scripture that says "My tongue is like the pen of a ready writer..." (Psalms 45:1) I close this chapter with this, what will you inscribe upon your heart and the hearts of others when you release your words? Your words are SEED, and you shall have what you SAY. Write the story of your life with positive words of love, of strength, and with the promises of God. May you always speak life, love, peace, and power into the lives of others, the universe will thank you!

Chapter 8

FAMILY IS NOT LIMITED TO BLOOD

"The power of FAMILY is in each and every one of us. No two families may look or operate the same, but they are still a FAMILY. The lifeblood of our communities is FAMILY, and communities shape the hearts of our world."
~ Tammy Wicks

A few years ago, I wrote a post on my blog on Veteran's Day. I decided to reprint this post for my first published book as it is worth repeating. You will read multiple times my references to my friends and family that are such a part of who I am. My parents raised me well, and I always like to add, however, I grew up in the Air Force. This chapter while short, is a shout out to every service member who crossed my path, you know who you are. I salute you and would not have made it without you and the Grace of God! You've been kind to my children and me, and I am so thankful.

I have dedicated an entire Chapter to Friendships in another volume of this book, but I wanted to include this chapter separately to demonstrate the camaraderie of the Military Family. Moreover, I wanted to emphasize that family to me is not limited to a DNA double-helix, but it is woven together with sacrifices of the heart, assignment after assignment. I called my blog post "Forever Friendships":

As this Veteran's Day comes to a close, I have been reflecting on some of the best friendships I have known in my life. My "Military Family" is one that is so special, so unique, and organically a part of what it means to be a part of our great Armed Forces. I don't know how I would have survived for over 21 years without my Military Family. I say to people all of the time this: "You are with those you work with every day awake, longer than you are with your family every day. These are precious & lifelong connections.

We don't have to talk every day, or every month, but the strong connection remains. We know each other's spouses, watch each other's children come into the world, become their babysitters, their "Aunts" & "Uncles," and follow them through adulthood. We work long hours, we travel together, and we house-sit for each other. We support the families that are holding it down until their military member returns home. We become each other's confidants, supporters, mentors, and genuine friends. We fill in the gaps for each other to ensure the mission is fulfilled. So many selfless and repeated acts of kindness have been overwhelmingly received, it's simply amazing!!!

For me, the friendships have transcended new assignments, various moves, our blue uniform, and our retirements. They are solid connections that I truly cherish. To all my friends throughout the years, THANK YOU for your mentoring, your support, your encouragement, your chastisement, your correction, your confidence, and your love. I appreciate each and every one of you and I am so glad to call you my Military Family. Thank you for your servant leadership and for your examples of true FRIENDSHIP & FAMILY. I am richly blessed. Lastly, thank you for your service!! your correction, your confidence, and your love. I appreciate each and every one of you and I am so glad to call you my Military Family.

One of my quotes is, "my parents raised me, but I grew up in the Air Force." The US Military is such a big part of my life I had to ensure I included a nod in my first book. I loved the military, my friends, and my friends who became my family! I don't know what I would do without my family, the one that God placed me in and the one that He created for me as I traveled around the world. I am so very thankful to each of you as you have contributed to my growth and development, the good, the bad, and the ugly.

Thank you from the depths of my soul for your love, support, advice, and holding me accountable. May God bless the continued foundation of FAMILY!!

Chapter 9

TAKE CARE OF YOURSELF

The Lord is my strength and shield. I trust him with all my heart. He helps me, and my heart is filled with joy. I burst out in songs of thanksgiving. Psalms 28:7

I dedicate this chapter to every person who feels like they don't have enough time. Enough time for what? Time for yourself. As adults, it's effortless to come up with reasons to find other things to do other than to take time for self. I know my own personal testimony is that when I began having children, and I only have two, I felt guilty at times. I felt guilty for spending money to do things like to get my hair done or to get my nails done or just to go away on a trip. These things brought me a little bit of anxiety because I could always find that the time spent doing something just for me could be time spent doing something for my children. Or the money spent doing something just for me could be money spent doing something for my children. I just always made an excuse not to do it.

When I did that, I found myself also feeling overwhelmed, under-appreciated, and overly stressed. So I had an epiphany one day. It started when I was on maternity leave after having my son, and I was in Hawaii. I found that walking to drop my daughter off at school while he was in the stroller while I was on maternity leave gave me great joy. It was refreshing, I felt renewed in the air, the atmosphere, the scenery...and I enjoyed it!! Of course, it was doing wonders for my

physical body, the exercise was great, but it did something for my

emotional being as well. So I decided to keep walking. I was home for

a little over nine weeks, and that became a part of my routine unless it

was inclement weather. It was something that comforted me, and I

found that I needed comfort more than I was willing to admit. Then I

asked myself, "If I can do this and be comforted, what else can I find

to do just for me?" I picked back up my journals and restarted writing.

All of my friends recognized that I was in a season, and while I

didn't quite name that season, they identified it. I will call it my

"Out of Balance" season of my life. I had an active and wonderful

4-year-old, a newborn, a career, I was finishing my Bachelor's Degree,

and I couldn't pull it all together some days. All of my friends, near and

far, were so caring, compassionate, and very open about some of my

challenges. They shared their own experiences, they babysat my child or

children to allow me time to myself, but most importantly, they listened

to me.

"Out of balance" was undoubtedly the words to describe my

season, but the beautiful end of my story was that every season comes

to an end. (Ecclesiastes 3:1-8) I also began to realize that these seasons

were necessary for growth. The cutting away, the goodbyes, the new

babies, the latest jobs, the "new" and "old" are necessary change agents

for growth and "the better" in your life. Moreover, I learned that

seasons in your life will always change. It is part of our development;

it's part of our process, fortification, and purification! At times you

need to be alone with God, refresh, relax, take accountability and

inventory for what's going on in your life and allow God to guide you

regarding the necessary adjustments.

So as I began on the road of disciplining myself to find comfort

and peace again, God showed up once again in an unexpected way. I

had an elect group of friends and coworkers in Hawaii, and

unbeknownst to me, they had been watching. I guess others saw the

stress, the imbalance, the awkward footing in me. It was almost as if

God spoke directly to their hearts about my condition and season and

used them to step in. These elect friends mean the world to me to this

very day. We don't talk every day, we are miles apart, but it is like we never missed a beat whenever we connect.

There were two significant encounters that I'll explain: my breaking, and my healing. I was going to get my hair done one night at a friend's home and they are still today, like family. I had my daughter, her little friend who was her buddy, and my baby boy Daniel. It was a Friday night, so I stopped by a drive-through for dinner and looked forward to putting another hectic week behind me. I jumped out of the car at her house with the girls, went inside her home, and immediately she said, "oh, where is Lil' Man tonight.?" For about two minutes, I had left my son in the back seat of my car alone. I freaked out! He was fast asleep as I had left him, but the fact was, I had left him. So I empathize with the parents who accidentally leave their child for a brief moment.

Now, let me just say when I went back inside the house, I was so ashamed, I was an absolute MESS!!! My daughter and her friend were playing in the living room and eating their fast-food in front of the TV where my friends had made them comfortable. However, just a few rooms over, I was broken. I cried, they consoled, but it took me a minute to understand and accept that I needed help adjusting to my

new season. This night could have ended in several different ways, one

of them with me having my parenting abilities legally questioned.

Instead, God's grace stepped in once again, and as He always does, He

covered me. The Holy Spirit immediately quickened my friend's heart

to inquire about Daniel, and the situation was restored, but my heart

wasn't. Thank you Ty & Joye, I am so glad I was at your home when

all of that happened. Thank you for standing in the gap for me and my

babies in my time of need.

Now my healing. One of my friends used to like to plan

Saturdays with the kids and do different things. Some were simple.

Others were a little involved, like the trip to the Big Island of Hawaii.

Nevertheless, I went and enjoyed every moment as these adventures

pulled me out of my comfort zone. My daughter Tiara especially loved

these times because she had other little girls for playtime. My time in

Hawaii would have never been the same without these ladies and their

precious babies. Each of you knows who you are, and I thank you

from the depths of my spirit for your friendship, love, and support through the years.

Back to these wonderful ladies, they arranged for me to have a Spa Day. I didn't know anything about it. If I recall, it was under the guise of going to a yard sale or something, again, with Connie and crew you never knew! I just knew it would be a typical Saturday, so I was eager to go, Daniel laying still in a baby carrier, Tiara right behind me. However, when we pulled up to the house, Connie told the kids to stay in the car. She and Tonya gave me a little bag with some toiletries and slowly explained that it was not a yard sale, what they were doing, and that they would be back in a couple of hours to get me. I stood there and thought of every reason that it was a bad idea, "But...but...what about...", I just babbled. However, they had thought of every single thing. I couldn't say no.

Connie Sue, TLee, and Chief Debbie (as I affectionately call them) had arranged the sweetest experience. I was overwhelmed with emotion, and the spa was in a home. She took me by the hand and ushered me into a fabulous and relaxing experience. "What had I said or done that provoked them into doing this for me?" "What did they see?" I don't have time for things like this?" "My children are going to wonder where I am at." "I hope they didn't spend too much." My mind was racing, and she just said this to me, "Relax, forget about everything else, and take this time for you." I just cried and cried and cried...and cried. The release was so incredibly powerful that it overtook me.

She asked me to change because she had a bath prepared with rose petals and special oils, the music was as soothing as her voice, and her words deeply pierced my spirit. At that moment, it did not matter that she was a complete stranger; something heavy broke off of me that day. It was mental, emotional, and spiritual all at the same time. There were no other clients, just me, her, and God. I have never found a place like that, and I probably never will. After a lot of crying and cleansing came the rest, and I was perhaps snoring (loudly) while she massaged me, but again, I was free; I did not care. I was at peace.

Make a promise to yourself that you will always take care of you. Everyone needs help sometimes, care enough about yourself to seek help when needed. If you are ever in a position in your life where you fail to acknowledge or recognize that you need to take care of yourself, make sure you have a strong circle, whether they are friends or family. This circle will do the same thing that mine did, they recognized that I was out of balance. I believe by the Spirit of God, they gently set me on a road of health, healing and peace. My friends will never know the depth of what they did for me that day. They do now. Connie, Tonya, Chief Debbie, and anyone else involved in that "spa moment", I will forever thank you. This moment was a significant awakening and I will never forget it.

Chapter 10

PRESSING THROUGH

I'm not saying that I have this all together, that I
have it made. But I am well on my way, reaching
out for Christ, who has so wondrously reached out
for me. Friends, don't get me wrong: By no means
do I count myself an expert in all of this, but I've
got my eye on the goal, where God is beckoning
us onward—to Jesus. I'm off and running, and I'm
not turning back. Phil 3:12-14

When I thought about this chapter and what to name it, I didn't want to be overly complicated because that's not who I am. But I did want the importance of the last chapter of Volume I to represent who I was, what I have learned, and what will continue to be a part of my life. I like to be significantly specific in my discussions, but this lesson was too important to skim over. So this last chapter is very appropriately named, PRESSING THROUGH!

When my children were young and ever since they were old enough to understand, my response to so many of their questions would be, "Press through." This response was universal for so many of their situations, whether in their sports activities or if they felt too sick to go to school, or perhaps they were dealing with a tough challenge at school, my answer would be the same. No matter the challenge, the words "get over it" did not work, but the statement "press through" struck a different chord within; so, peppered with love, I found myself saying it often.

I balanced between my daughter, who never wanted to miss anything school for any reason, even if she was sick, and my son, who was so creative and came up with interesting reasons for missing at least a part of the day in elementary school. My daughter had perfect attendance from the sixth grade through to her senior year in high school - perfect! I take about 10% credit for this (stop laughing, Tiara)! In all seriousness, this was her accomplishment all the way. However, my daughter understood and still understands the importance of pressing through. She's very self-motivated and has all of her goals etched out for herself. Her achievement does not mean that she was never tired or struggling with being under the weather; she just had a mindset that she would not miss school. She always chose to press through!

I did not raise my children to be average, as that is not how my parents raised my siblings and me. So I applied my parent's same loving, firm hands to my children. I sought advice from friends and family often...I still do. More importantly, I sought God for instruction, wisdom, and strength regarding how to raise my children...I always will.

Parenting can be challenging if you do it the right way...and I give it my all. As I said, whenever they felt sick or felt like they had a little cold, I would tell them to press through. One of my favorite lines, which I am sure they grew tired of hearing, was, "If you don't go to school today just because you feel a little cold coming on, what will happen when you grow up and start working? Are you going to call out every time you feel sick or have a sniffle? PRESS THROUGH!"

I distinctly recall when my son was a kindergartner, and he was limping a bit one morning when we were leaving for school. I asked a few questions but he explained, "Mama, I am ok. I probably slid too much when I was playing soccer this weekend." My GIANT son Daniel thought that every time he attempted a goal, it required sliding--too funny to watch! He is an entirely different child in his own right and very intelligent like his sister, very confident, skillful, loving, and compassionate. He is more similar to his sister than he will ever admit.

I thank God for both of my incredibly blessed children; however, Tiara is very methodical and pragmatic. Daniel processes things in a completely different way. HE has to understand and process it, then he can move forward with the plans. I would often think he would make a pretty good lawyer or agent because he is always negotiating with me. So back to the morning of the limp, I tried to inspect his body physically, and he said, "Mama, I am feeling a little sore, but I'm pressing through, I'm pressing through." He was persistent. It was a Friday morning, and I will never forget it. I received an email from his teacher before I went to pick him up from the after-school program, and she expressed some concerns about his limp. She explained that it slowed him down all day, but he was persistent, and at one point, she picked him up and carried him. When I picked him up, once again, Daniel downplayed it and told me it was from soccer, and he was fine, and he showed no signs of distress at that time. About 5 am the next morning, Daniel came into my room screaming and crying, telling me how bad he was hurting in his groin area, so I scooped him up, dropped my daughter at my Mom's house, and settled in for a long ER visit. They immediately checked him (thank God and 'shout out' to Martin Army Hospital in Fort Benning, Georgia). He changed into a gown, and when the doctor performed the physical exam, Daniel was suffering from an incarcerated hernia.

After a helicopter ride to a Children's Hospital and an angelic visitation (another story for another book), Daniel had emergency s surgery and was better than ever. As his mother, I felt horrible. Did I press him too much? Was he too young to understand "pressing through"? After every event played out in that situation, Daniel was able to experience God on another level. To this day, he remembers significant events of that weekend. But, when I look back on that event, I wonder how things would have played out if Daniel did not press through? God's faithfulness shined through in a way that I could not have taught him, all because he dared to PRESS! Time and time again, what I have discovered when pressing through is that you find out who YOU are, not just what others say about you. In essence, if you stop to pay attention, you will find out who God says you are. Pressing through is also about who you become after you are on the other side. A lot is going on in the process of the press.

In the world around us, there's a lot that's happening. We press through in our careers daily, and we press through things going on in our home life, with our spouses, our children. We plow through

various financial issues and multiple other adversities. In other words,

we stay in the PRESS. We have rough days, yet we have to come home

and smile for our children through the stress because we have to be

present and available to hear all about their day and their challenges.

We have overwhelming days, but as soon as we hit the door, our

spouse needs to decompress or talk about something that we may not

feel like talking about at that moment, but we sit down, listen, and we

press through. We all need someone, too. When we need to vent or

unpack, it may not happen when we need it because of every other task

on our "to do" lists, at least that is my world, minus the spouse, but I

continue to press.

Without a doubt, I can say with all conviction and truth that I

could have never imagined the person I am today without God's grace

and faith in Him. My faith has carried me through every season when I

was mentally, emotionally, psychologically, and sometimes physically

challenged. My faith is the fuel that gives me the fortitude to press

through. I look back and say to myself, "God, if you brought me through that, then surely you can bring me through this thing as well!" That is when I dig down deep and remember what Paul says in Philippians chapter 3:14. Paul says, "I press towards the mark, (the goal), for the prize of the high call in Jesus Christ." I was stuck on this scripture for years because I didn't understand the "press." What was the true meaning of the press for Paul? I believe Paul understood that there was a more significant responsibility, something bigger than himself, and he was not going to let anything get in his way. He was about his Father's business.

Paul did not care about who he was before, that was a part of his testimony. Paul looked at the new thing God was doing and how God was using him in that season. In reading this I was inspired, I knew that I had to mature and grow, and as my Mama says, "when you know better, you do better." There is a bigger picture, more significant challenges, and new levels in God that I need to get to! What must I do? Forget those things that are behind me, and press towards the mark, in every area of my life!

When I awake and thank God, no matter how I think, feel, or

look, I have to get myself in the right posture and frame of mind to press through the day's challenges, because they are present. That challenge may knock me down, but it won't take me out, I believe that! I believe what Psalms 23 says, and I have confidence knowing that Jesus is walking with me, no matter what, in the valleys or on the mountain, He is there! God said he would never leave us or forsake us, just look to the scriptures. We are never alone. (Heb 13:5) God's Word promises us that we have an advocate in Jesus, (1 John 2:1), even when we miss the mark, His grace is covering us. We don't have time to be ashamed, we have to repent, reset, and press! I know where my strength and my help comes from, it comes from God. (Neh 8:10, Psalm 138:3) I can go on and on all day about Jesus, but my point here is we don't have to do this life alone. We don't have to press alone, we have the ULTIMATE PRESS in Him.

The key here is when we are going through anything, God has given us the ability to press. I can just envision Jesus by my side holding my hand and walking with me; The Holy Spirit gently guiding me with a soft wind at my back; and God's Word lighting my path. I'm pressing because The Triune God is right here with me, and they are right there with every one of us daily. I believe that pressing through brings about God's divine timing and divine order. So I will keep pressing through, how about you?

In Conclusion

CONSIDER THESE THINGS...

For with God nothing [is or ever] shall be
impossible." Luke 1:37

So as I close this last chapter of Volume 1, I want to leave you with a few thoughts that resonate and are on "repeat" in my mind and heart. They are solid, tried, and true:

- Confess The Word of God over your life daily, it will change the perspective that you see EVERYTHING through!

- Remember that you are <u>multitudes of amazing</u>, so walk in the confidence that God has made you EXACTLY who <u>He wanted</u> you to be!

- God is not going to allow us to stay stuck in the press. He's going to use our tests and trials as stair-steps to our next level in Him. Just keep moving, keep learning, and keep growing!

- Forgive yourself for anything in your past that sounds like failure, lack, or not good enough. God has called you to be successful, to be more than a conqueror, and to live in abundance!

- In every season of obscurity, God is with you. Listen to what He is saying.

- In every season of struggle, God is developing and training you, to pass the test He is giving.

- In every season of a battle, God is teaching you how to fight in the Spirit, don't invoke your natural weapons for a spiritual battle.

- An open-mind and an open-heart are the best fertilizer for dreams to take root and grow! Clear out the stuff that has you captive!

- KNOW YOUR WORTH and VALUE Y-O-U, it took me too long to learn this lesson but when I saw myself as God saw me, my eyes and heart opened up!

- When you don't receive that promotion, or get selected for a specific job, or a relationship does not work out, or maybe something did not go your way, trust that it was not supposed to work out that way. God always knows exactly what YOU need, and that will always be what works out best for YOU! Even when you don't agree, just TRUST HIM...period...the end...Amen!

- God has so many blessings for you, press, pray, and patiently wait on the manifestation in your life! It will be worth the wait!

- God has impeccable timing, just trust Him!

- No one can dream YOUR dream bigger than you because God gave it to you. So DREAM INCREDIBLY BIG!! If not now, when?

- In every season of abundance, which is God's intended daily state for us, be faithful, thankful, and charitable. This will create

  room for your next wave of blessings.

- Whatever you make happen for someone else God will make happen for you, so rejoice, yours is on the way!

- "We" may have been "them" once, be careful how judgment is passed.

- Laugh, live, and do what brings you joy!

- Finish what you start...no matter how long it takes...just do it!

- Be a life-long learner in every area of your life, no one has "arrived" until you go to meet Jesus!

- Life can be a bit of a roller coaster...steady in places...but a bit upside down at times. Find your balance...maintain it...and when "life happens", just repeat and press!

- If you are doing it right, parenthood, marriage, relationships... they can all be hard. What can you do? Do whatever it takes to MASTER them...pray, seek counseling, read books, attend workshops, be open to the fact that people have climbed these mountains before you. God put them here to help all of us out. Seek to Master those tough things in your life and find your way to peace and joy, it's our strength!

- **Love like God loves**.....you will experience life in an entirely different way.

1 Corinthians 13:4-10 (Message Bible)

If I give everything I own to the poor and

even go to the stake to be burned as a martyr,

but I don't love, I've gotten nowhere. So, no

matter what I say, what I believe, and what I do,

I'm bankrupt without love.

Love never gives up.

Love cares more for others than for self.

Love doesn't want what it doesn't have.

Love doesn't strut, Doesn't have a swelled head,

Doesn't force itself on others, Isn't always "me first,"

Doesn't fly off the handle,

Doesn't keep score of the sins of others,

Doesn't revel when others grovel,

Takes pleasure in the flowering of truth,

Puts up with anything,

Trusts God always,

Always looks for the best,

Never looks back,

But keeps going to the end.

Love never dies...

Love like God loves

ACKNOWLEDGEMENTS & INDEFINTE THANK YOUS...

Do not withhold good from those to whom it is due, when it is in your power to act. If you have the power to do good, do it as unto the Lord. God bless and do tell the Lord thank you.
Proverbs 3:27

ACKNOWLEDGEMENTS & INDEFINITE THANKS

First, it is impossible for me to remember everyone because I have been so blessed and enriched by so many of you over the years. I say in advance to anyone that I overlooked, please know that I love you, appreciate you, and I thank you.

To my Lord and Savior Jesus Christ...not as a cliche but as my LIFE, my God, my EVERYTHING!! Without God, there would be no me. Worthy of ALL praise does not begin to describe where You are in my heart. You are THE ONLY one who knows ALL of my story...with that said, thank you for still loving me through it all with your grace, mercy, and loving kindness. I don't deserve your kind of matchless unconditional love! I swell up with tears as I write, THANK YOU JESUS for loving me, never giving up on me, and anointing me with your gifts and talents to show the world your love, your grace, mercy, compassion, and your favor.

Next, to my precious children. Yes, this book is dedicated to them in part, but I could not thank everyone else without thanking them. They know Mommy, and they see more of me than anyone else other than God. They know the good, the bad, and the ugly, the private hurts, and the many failures. But they love me in spite of anything and without judgement. I cannot wait for the indelible marks that you will both make all over the world! I love you both so much, I love on higher and deeper levels because of you both. I believe on another level because what I have seen God do in your lives. I hope more because of everything I want for the two of you. As I say to you all the time, "go with Jesus!"

Next, my involuntary "Creative Consultants" Tiara, Daniel, Patrina, Obsidian, Beverly, DeAja, Nykia, Stephanie, and Dwayne (Si), thank you so much for the million reviews that you completed graciously and without reservation. I will be calling on your services for the future as you know I am not fancy, so I need your eyes and opinions!

Next, I've given you a glimpse into who my family is in this book through stories, but I want to expressly and genuinely thank my late father who had a huge part in my journey. To my mother who has always been my biggest fan. I couldn't ask God for a better mother &

father. I thank God for you both for supporting me, depositing into me, for correcting me, and most importantly for ensuring that I was brought up in the fear and admonition of the Lord! Thank you for your unconditional and abundant love, and keen wisdom. I love you and I thank you so much for life!

To my beloved siblings, thank you so much for allowing me to be me. I couldn't be where I'm at today in my life doing the things I love to do without all of you. Each of you is a gift and a blessing to me and my children. Thank you for motivating me, for driving me, for pushing me, for advising me, for putting me in my place when needed, but most of all for loving me unconditionally. I appreciate each of you so much, and from the depths of my soul I thank God for you all!

To my nieces and nephews, such beautiful and intelligent adults, young adults, and children with amazing futures. I am so proud of you all & I pray that you come to understand the unlimited blessings that are in store for you, just tap into them! You make me one proud Auntie over and over again! I love you, keep doing good in the world, and keep Jesus at the center of it all! Special hugs & kisses to "my baby," my precious great-nephew, Aiden Hundley.

To all the rest of my relatives near and far, if I tried to start naming you, the list would be a book all by itself! Love to you all, Mason & Peterkin alike! I thank God for placing me in this strong & loving family, and crazy too, but all love!

To my current Pastor of The Bridge Church Columbus, in Columbus, Georgia, Pastor Vince Allen. You are a great man of faith and you have taught me so much, I am forever grateful. To his wife, my First Lady, Beatrice Casiano-Allen, also known as Sweet Lady Bea, thank you for being you! You are LOADED, can't wait for you to start unpacking all of those gifts! I love you both so much, thank you for being the leaders, mentors, and the selfless Pastors that you are, always serving with love. Shout out to The BridgeNation!!

To every Bishop, Pastor, Chaplain, Minister, Brother or Sister whom I've had the privilege & honor to cross paths with, there are too many of you, but I thank you for your presence in my life. My path to God and with God is because you have shown me what it is to build one another up in our most Holy Faith and bear each other's burdens!

Through faith, patience, and prayer you loved me through it all, thank you all, 100-fold return blessing to you and yours. Very special thanks to Chap Ashford, Chap Burrell & Natalie, Chap Sanders & Lisa Sanders for watching over my soul as my former Pastors.

To those that I can call or text day or night and you always have time to provide prayer, encouragement, correction, and you never leave me without a prophetic or inspiring Word from God. You are anointed to care for me and mine, and have done so selflessly! Words can't express the connection, the love and respect I have for all of you. You mean to me because only God knows what each of you have done, tremendous thanks and may God grant you all every desire of your hearts. You have never steered me wrong, you walk with God with true humility and grace, and you are so full of compassion and love for others. With a full and sincere heart, I thank you all: Bishop Ernest & Brenda Carradine, Bishop Yvonne Jones, Apostle Kevin & Cowenda Jefferson, Rev (Dr, Chief) Filbert Martin, Min Brenda Traylor, Elder Janis Zimmerman, Min Dahene Burwell, Min Maurice James & Patrina James, Min Ty Alston & Joye Alston.

To my special friends who are also like family, and the Godparents of my children, Doug Jones, Bishop Yvonne Jones, Uncle Maurice (Mo) & Aunt Patrina "Treen Treen" James. You all have been miraculous blessings!! You have blessed my children and me beyond measure and we are so thankful to have you in our lives. You all have been spiritual pillars that have held us up, emotionally, spiritually, financially, and everything in between. I love you all & thank you!

To Prophetess Cynthia Steele, I thank God for you and your husband, Apostle Steele. You both were so impactful in my life. As one example, in the Summer of 1998, you spoke a prophetic word over my life before I left for Korea. You were very specific in your prophecy about me writing when no one else in the room knew that I was in my secret place writing, but God knew. A few years ago I reached out to you because I thought, is it too late? Did I miss something? But you assured me that God's Word will not return to Him void. Over two decades later, here it is and it's only the beginning. Thank you for lighting a fire that I was unable to fully understand myself. I love you & cherish you both so much.

To my special friends who I've had the privilege of calling friends for multiple years, some for over two decades. You are more than friends, you are my family. You have been a "village" for my children, you have been with me through laughs, tears, defining moments, significant life events. You have been a consistent presence in my life, THANK YOU ALL, and you know that I love you. In no particular order as I am blessed to have you all in my life: Beverly Tucker, Dwayne Silas, Demetrius & Kathy Jones, Kathy McCullough, Kenneth "K-Rob" & Mercedes Robinson, Tonya Lee, Prophetess Janet Wells, Mia Wells, Tyhisha & Jermaine Dupree, Ursula & Wayde Hamilton, Jim Wilson, Carla Holbrook, Timothy Domek (my brother from another mother) & Kathy Jaeger, Chief Debbie Stocks & Phillip (aka, Buttercup), Lisa Willis, Michael & Jeannie Kanaby, Christina (CAAS) Austin-Smith & Brandon, Col Pamela Stevenson, Col Ted & Kathy Fink, Lisa Willis, Mel Charles, Connie Giersch, Kim (T-Ross) & Ananias Ross, Kendrell Smith, Ty & Joye Alston, Remoh "Mo" Thompson, Tommy Spikes, Jujuana Howard, LaTanya & Dennis Brigman (aka

"The Brinkmans"), The "Graceites" of GFCC, Bridgett Martin,

Brenda Law, Rudy & Dr. Chief Denise Lewis, Dexter "DKG" Grier,

Cilynthia Blount - who often reminded me to stay on task with writing,

Tenise Lovett, Rev & Mrs. Liz Nuckles, Renata Mills, Chuck Burkhart,

Ms. Pat Turner, Brenda Traylor & Tray, Crystal McLean-Radcliff,

"EPA" Rose Palmer & Madison, Stephanie Hammonds (with a "d"),

and Denise Sharpton.

Thank you to those who have led me and supervised me, past a

present, to my work families over the years, to those who still connect

and mentor me. Special thanks to Rob Hadden and Dave Kelley,

you afforded me a transition when I retired and have mentored me

through it all. Thank you for your professional and personal advice,

and for your unwavering support, for picking up the phone when I

call, or returning my texts, still guiding me as you always have.

Blessings to you and your families now and always.

Thank you to the Air Force JAG & Paralegal Community all

across this world whom I had the privilege to serve with, there are too

many to name. I will never forget any of you! Special thanks to

"The Chiefs", To The Hickam Family, The Fairchild Family, The Osan Family--OMG - those Sunday Dinners, The Eglin Family, The Mountain Home Family, The Ramstein Family, and The AFJAGS Family, and The AU/Maxwell Family. You are all a part of my story and you made it an amazing, wonderful journey, thank you.

Last but not least, to the village that I was a part of, and who helped raise me over the years, I love you and thank you. To The Lyde Family, The Miller Family, The Montgomery/Rothwell Family, The Douglas Family, Cousin/Aunt Dee Smith & Family, and to the "Cordova Crew", love you all dearly & deeply. We are _forever_ family!

About The Author

ABOUT THE AUTHOR

Tammy is a devoted mother of two anointed children, Tiara and Daniel, and a proud retired Air Force Veteran of 21 years. Her passion is writing, and she has been doing so privately all of her life. In the past few years, she's felt the push from God to share her gift with the world. She also loves to create, design, and express her heart, and she helps others do the same. This book is the first of many on this journey. As the CEO, Owner, and Operator of her own publishing company, Tidan Publishing. Tammy understands it is her God-mandated purpose to inspire people's hearts to believe more than what their eyes can see through words, one word at a time, through published works.

OTHER TITLES BY TAMMY WICKS COMING SOON

FaithFull
A 31-day journey dedicated to experiencing God's Faithfulness

Even Though I Am Not There...I Am Always Here, **Vol 2**

Made in the USA
Monee, IL
04 April 2021